WRITTEN BY
JO NELSON
ILLUSTRATED BY
YISHAN LI

GREAT SPACE EXPLORERS

Contents

OXFORD
UNIVERSITY PRESS

Copernicus and Armstrong

For more than a thousand years, people have been exploring space in different ways – people like the astronomer Nicolaus Copernicus and the astronaut Neil Armstrong.

What a trip! You should have come with me, Copernicus.

But I'm already a great explorer!

You've not even left Earth, let alone walked on the Moon like me!

Admit it, Armstrong. Astronauts like you have only explored the teeniest part of space.

I explored much further with my observations.

We know lots about the Solar System today, but it took hundreds of space explorers and thousands of years to discover what's actually out there.

Saturn

Jupiter

Uranus

Sun

Venus

Earth

Mercury

Neptune

Mars

Before clocks and calendars, people just used the Sun and the Moon to chart the passage of time.

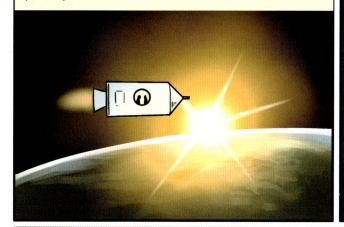

For example, it's roughly a month from one full Moon to the next.

However, as time went on, people saw other links in the night sky.

In 2000 BC, the Ancient Egyptians used the annual appearance of a specific star to predict when the river Nile would flood and bring precious water to their fields.

The star's appeared! The river's going to flood! Spread the word!

Ancient astronomers found more patterns and links in the night sky.

Their careful studies of the sky also began to unlock the secrets of space.

Shi Shen and Gan De

Shi Shen and Gan De were the first named astronomers to compile **catalogues** of the stars.

China, 350 BC

...119, 120, 121 ... I've plotted the positions of 121 stars!

Excellent! Knowing exactly where the stars are will help us keep time and make predictions about the sky.

In the King's court ...

Shi Shen, can you calculate when the next **eclipse** of the Sun will come?

Leave it with me, mighty ruler.

In ancient times, eclipses frightened people. They were seen as a warning of bad things to come.

Working out when this will next happen is tricky.

That might do it!

Successfully predicting an eclipse made a ruler appear powerful and strong.

Don't panic. Our ruler said this would happen.

Our ruler truly is wise.

Shi Shen and Gan De also studied the planets. There are five planets visible in the night sky without a telescope.

They look like stars, only they don't twinkle.

And they move in strange ways. Let's keep a detailed record of their movements.

Gan De even spotted one of **Jupiter's** moons.

If I use a tree to block out the light of that planet, I can see another tiny shape beside it.

Gan De didn't actually know it was a moon, but it was one of many important observations that he wrote down and shared.

Shi Shen and Gan De's observations were used by other astronomers for many hundreds of years.

Shi Shen even had a crater on the Moon named after him.

Aristarchus of Samos

Where shall we go next?

How about Ancient Greece? I want you to meet a personal hero of mine …

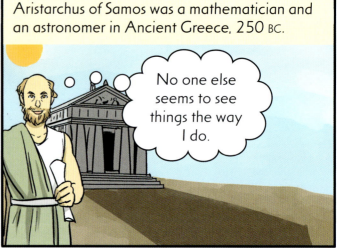

Aristarchus of Samos was a mathematician and an astronomer in Ancient Greece, 250 BC.

No one else seems to see things the way I do.

Other people see the Sun move across the sky and think it must be moving around Earth.

But I think Earth is actually spinning on itself and moving around the Sun.

Around a hundred years earlier, the great Ancient Greek thinkers Plato and Aristotle had described their model of the universe.

Here's Earth, stationary at the centre.

The Sun and planets move around Earth in perfect circles.

It seemed so obvious, everyone thought it had to be true.

Well, nearly everyone: Aristarchus wasn't convinced.

If the planets are moving in regular circles around Earth then why do they sometimes seem bigger and brighter? And why do they move in an irregular pattern?

Don't you see, Earth is actually moving around the Sun!

Impossible!

Earth feels pretty still to me!

The stars are actually distant suns! The universe is far bigger than we can imagine!

Rubbish! Liar!

But he was right!

I know, but the truth is sometimes hard to believe.

Hipparchus of Nicaea

So who are we meeting next?

Another Ancient Greek – possibly the greatest of all the ancient astronomers.

Greek island of Rhodes, 130 BC

It's a perfect night for stargazing.

Hipparchus of Nicaea spent most of his adult life observing and researching the Sun and the night sky.

He calculated the length of a **lunar month**.

That's 29 days, 12 hours, 44 minutes and 2½ seconds.

He also worked out the length of a **solar year** – well, almost.

Hipparchus's calculation was 6 minutes too long. A solar year is really 365 days, 5 hours, 48 minutes and 46 seconds.

There were no telescopes to help Hipparchus view the night sky. The instruments he used were the **astrolabe** …

… and the **quadrant**.

Hipparchus also got close to working out how far the Moon is from Earth.

I think it's 63 times the **radius** of Earth!

(It's actually 60.)

Not bad without a calculator! Shame he insisted on putting Earth at the centre of the Solar System, though. It's centuries before people get that one right.

Yes. In fact it gets worse before it gets better!

Claudius Ptolemy

Ancient Egypt, 150 AD

That's Ptolemy, the famous astronomer who made things worse.

Unfortunately, his model of our Solar System seemed so accurate that people used it for hundreds of years!

Finished at last! This collection of thirteen books will help people predict the positions of the Sun, Moon, planets and stars ... at any time!

It's all about the epicycles – circles within circles. That's how our universe goes round.

Using Ptolemy's model people could predict when and where a planet would appear in the night sky.

Of course at the centre of it all is our magnificent, stationary sphere: Earth.

Ptolemy's model wasn't seriously challenged for over 1300 years.

It must have taken someone special to prove Ptolemy wrong.

Well, I suppose I am rather special …

Of course – it was you, wasn't it?

Might have been.

Nicolaus Copernicus

If Ptolemy is correct, then tonight the bright star Aldebaran should be hidden by the Moon.

Copernicus decided to put Ptolemy's model to the test.

It's not! The model's wrong!

So what's really going on in space, I wonder …

It wasn't long before Copernicus read about Aristarchus – and the idea that the Sun, not Earth, was at the centre of the universe.

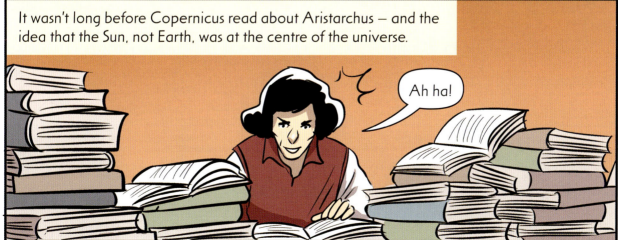

Ah ha!

Copernicus made many more calculations, testing out whether Aristarchus was right.

It must be true. But who's going to believe me?

He bought his own watchtower and continued his research, writing down his observations and improving his calculations.

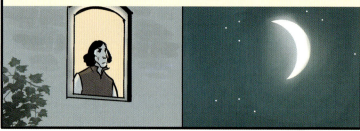

For many years, he kept his thoughts a secret, only sharing them with a few close friends.

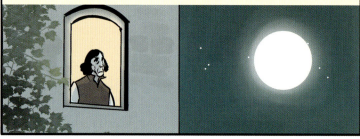

His friends tried to get him to tell others about his theories.

I don't know … people are going to laugh at me.

Not when they realize you're right!

Eventually he was persuaded to share his wisdom with the world.

Copernicus's book was published in 1543, causing great excitement, heated debates and public outrage.

Have you read this? Earth is no longer centre of the universe!

He should be locked up!

Copernicus is a genius.

Copernicus died that same year, aged 70.

People must have believed you when they read this?

A few, but the rest couldn't stomach the idea that Earth wasn't the centre of the universe … and in 1616 the book was banned!

Sorry to hear that.

At least I was able to see a copy of my book before I died.

Fortunately, all was not lost. New space explorers were entering the scene with an unquenchable thirst for the truth, including Galileo Galilei.

Galileo Galilei

Pisa, Italy, 1589: Galileo was Head of Mathematics at the University of Pisa aged only twenty-five. He was particularly interested in how objects move.

Aristotle says a heavy object falls more quickly than a lighter one, but I'm not so sure …

Ready, Galileo?

Now!

It's a draw!

Hmmm. I wonder what else the ancient thinkers got wrong.

One day, in 1604, something extraordinary happened in the night sky.

A new star! That shouldn't be possible!

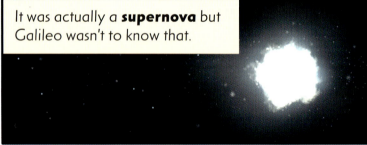

It was actually a **supernova** but Galileo wasn't to know that.

Aristotle and Ptolemy said the patterns of the universe never change, but this new star shows they're wrong. If only I could take a closer look at what's up there …

Fortunately, Hans Lippershey invented the telescope in 1608.

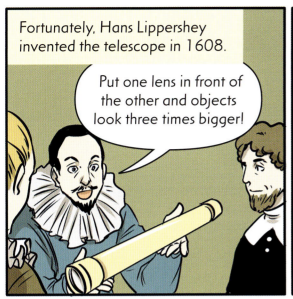

Put one lens in front of the other and objects look three times bigger!

Galileo heard about the design and immediately set about making his own, improved version.

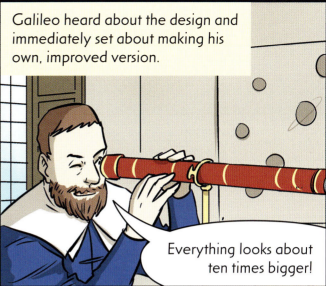

Everything looks about ten times bigger!

Galileo first demonstrated his telescope to a sea captain, from a tower in Venice.

Now look through this …

Nothing on the horizon.

I see a ship!

It's ingenious! Galileo, make me some telescopes for the navy and I will pay you handsomely.

Aye aye, Captain!

Galileo's telescope was a great success on Earth, but what could it reveal about space?

For weeks on end, Galileo became **nocturnal**, training his telescope on the stars and planets.

You have to see it to believe it!

Here's what he saw …

The Moon: Galileo was the first to discover that the Moon isn't a perfect sphere, but that it has mountains and craters like Earth!

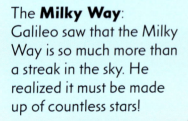

The **Milky Way**: Galileo saw that the Milky Way is so much more than a streak in the sky. He realized it must be made up of countless stars!

The moons of Jupiter: He also saw dots moving around Jupiter, just like the Moon moves around Earth … only he spotted that Jupiter has FOUR moons!

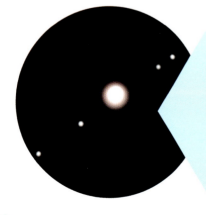

Hot off the press! The night sky like you've never seen it before!

Galileo wrote a paper about his discoveries and called it *Starry Messenger*. Everyone wanted to buy it.

The more Galileo saw, the more he agreed with Copernicus's model of the universe.

The planet Venus actually changes shape, from a small disk to a larger crescent. So it must be moving around the Sun.

Galileo wrote a book on his discoveries, including his arguments for the Sun being at the centre of our Solar System.

When the book was published in 1632, he expected more fame and fortune – but instead he was arrested …

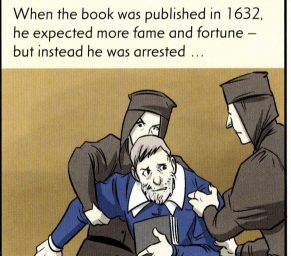

… and sentenced to life under house arrest!

What is my crime?

Claiming that Earth moves around the Sun.

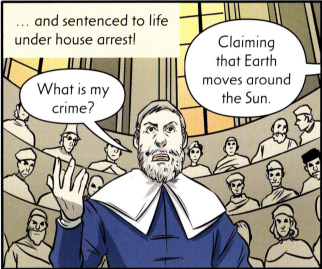

By then, Galileo was an old man. He lived his last years imprisoned in his own house.

What are you writing now?

A letter to my daughter.

OK. Just don't mention the Sun.

Poor Galileo. That's awful.

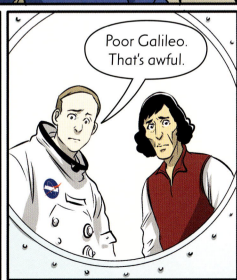

Williamina Stevens Fleming

It took several more decades for the Sun's position at the centre of our Solar System to be finally accepted …

… and for people to realize that our Solar System is just a tiny part of a much larger universe.

As the centuries went by, and telescopes improved, more and more space secrets were revealed.

Dundee, Scotland, 1871: Williamina Stevens was a very bright student and, by the age of fourteen, she was already teaching other students.

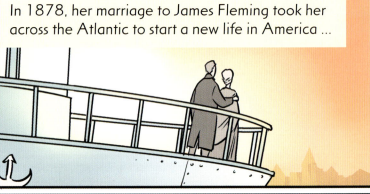

In 1878, her marriage to James Fleming took her across the Atlantic to start a new life in America …

… but within months, James had run off, leaving Williamina alone and pregnant with their first child.

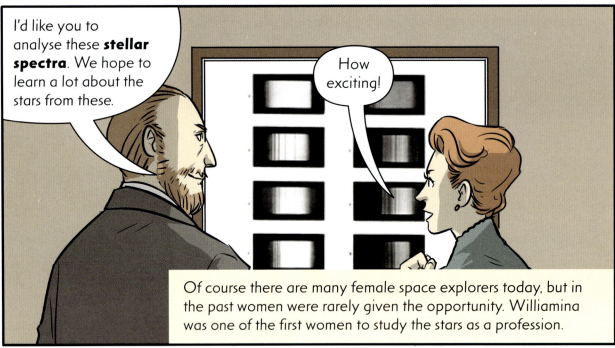

I'd like you to analyse these **stellar spectra**. We hope to learn a lot about the stars from these.

How exciting!

Of course there are many female space explorers today, but in the past women were rarely given the opportunity. Williamina was one of the first women to study the stars as a profession.

Nine years later …

I've catalogued more than ten thousand stars now …

But it's a mere splash in the ocean. There are millions more stars out there!

Then you'd better get some help.

So Williamina appointed a large team of women to work for her. Over the years they made some remarkable discoveries, including …

Ten novae …

A nova is a star that suddenly increases in brightness then gradually returns to its original state over a couple of months.

A nebula is a vast space cloud of dust and gas.

Over fifty nebulae …

And over 200 variable stars.

Variable stars vary in brightness, usually in a regular pattern.

Williamina was also the first person to discover white dwarf stars.

White dwarf stars are very hot, dense stars, nearing the end of their lifetime.

In 1906 Williamina Fleming was the first woman in America to be elected to the Royal Astronomical Society.

Yikes, Copernicus – I've just noticed the page number! At this rate, we'll never get to me!

Hmm. Let's see if this machine can go any faster.

Twentieth-century space explorers

Henrietta Swan Leavitt was one of Williamina Fleming's star researchers. In 1908 she made a groundbreaking discovery about the brightness of variable stars.

It's all about the **magnitude**!

This gave people a way to calculate how far away things are in the universe.

Edwin Hubble's study of variable stars in 1923 proved that the Milky Way is just one of many galaxies in the universe.

The light from distant stars tells us that the universe is still expanding!

Yuri Gagarin was the first man in space. He orbited Earth on 12th April 1961.

I see Earth. It is so beautiful!

Neil Armstrong was the first man to set foot on the Moon on 21st July 1969.

At last, there I am!

That's one small step for man, one giant leap for mankind.

Mae Jemison was the first African American woman in space.

Never be limited by other people's limited imaginations.

Maggie Aderin-Pocock is a British space scientist and television presenter.

I design powerful telescope and satellite parts. I always wanted to travel to the Moon, but through my work I've managed to explore so much further.

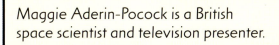

Maggie's reminded me – we really should take a look at the amazing rovers and space probes that are being sent to places no person has been before.

What's a space probe?

Robotic space explorers

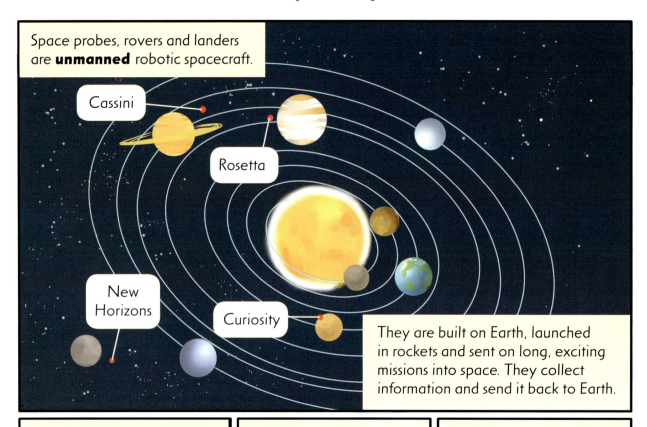

Space probes, rovers and landers are **unmanned** robotic spacecraft.

Cassini

Rosetta

New Horizons

Curiosity

They are built on Earth, launched in rockets and sent on long, exciting missions into space. They collect information and send it back to Earth.

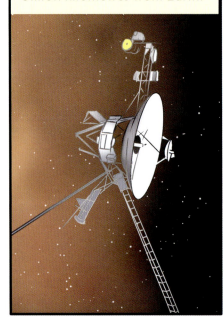

VOYAGER 1 was launched in 1977 and is the furthest spacecraft from Earth. It's now exploring the outer Solar System, around twenty billion kilometres from Earth!

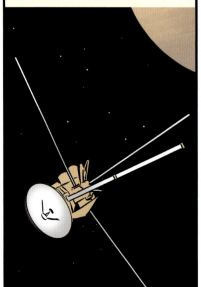

CASSINI was launched in 1997 and made **flybys** of Venus and Jupiter before becoming the first space probe to go into orbit around Saturn in 2004.

Cassini then released its lander module, HUYGENS, which successfully landed on Saturn's largest moon, Titan.

The space probe ROSETTA was launched in 2004. In 2014, it started orbiting a **comet**.

A few months later, it released its lander module, PHILAE, to examine the comet closer up.

CURIOSITY was launched in 2011. It is a robotic rover about the size of a car. It landed on Mars in 2012 and is investigating the climate and **geology** of the planet.

In 2015, NEW HORIZONS became the first space probe to make a flyby of the distant dwarf planet Pluto.

Wow, those robots are really showing us humans up!

Not at all. It's humans who have designed every single mission, down to the finest detail.

In fact, humans can now even live in space ...

The International Space Station was launched in 1998. The Space Station is orbiting Earth at a speed of 27600 km per hour – that's 7.66 km a second! It takes around 90 minutes for the Space Station to orbit Earth.

On board the Space Station, people and objects seem to be weightless due to the lack of gravity.

My name is Stephanie Wilson. I've been to the Space Station three times! While there, I had to learn how to exercise, eat, sleep and wash – all without gravity!

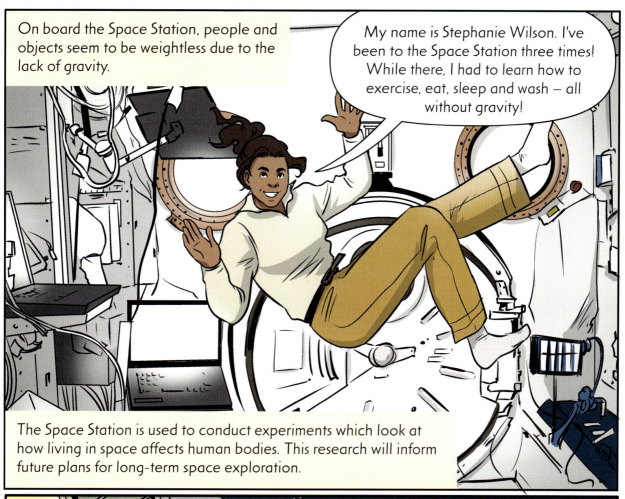

The Space Station is used to conduct experiments which look at how living in space affects human bodies. This research will inform future plans for long-term space exploration.

So what's next, Armstrong?

I guess that's up to the next generation. Building cities on Mars? Discovering life on other planets? Who knows what the great space explorers of the future will achieve!

Glossary

astrolabe　　an ancient instrument used to measure the positions of the Sun, Moon, stars and planets

catalogue　　a list

comet　　an icy lump that orbits the Sun

eclipse　　the Moon moving between Earth and the Sun

flyby　　a spacecraft flying close to something of interest in order to observe it

geology　　the study of the structure of a planet

Jupiter　　the largest planet in the Solar System, fifth away from the Sun

lunar month　　the time from one full Moon to the next

magnitude　　a number that shows the brightness of a star

Milky Way　　a huge galaxy that contains our Solar System

nocturnal　　active at night

quadrant　　an instrument used to measure angles

radius　　a straight line from the centre to the outer edge of a circle

solar year　　the time from an equinox (the time of year when day and night are equal in length) to the same equinox again. We now know this to be the time it takes for Earth to go once around the Sun.

stellar spectra　　light from stars, separated out for closer study

supernova　　an explosion happening in a very old star

unmanned　　without a crew on board

Index